WITHDRAWN

The Library of PIRATES™

Anne Bonny and Mary Read

Fearsome Female Pirates of the Eighteenth Century

Aileen Weintraub

The Rosen Publishing Group's
PowerKids Press™
New York

To my Daddymonster, who was the most fearless of them all

Published in 2002 by The Rosen Publishing Group, Inc.
 29 East 21st Street, New York, NY 10010

 First Edition

 Project Editors: Jennifer Landau, Jennifer Quasha
 Book Design: Michael Caroleo and Michael de Guzman
 Layout: Nicholas Sciacca

 Consultant: Ken Kinkor

 Photo credits: p. 4 (map) © Map Art; pp. 4, 16 © Mary Evans Picture Library; pp. 7, 8, 12, 15, 20 by
 Mica Angela Fulgium; pp. 7, 8 (inset) © North Wind Picture Archives; p. 11 (map) © Michael Maslan
 Historic Photographs/CORBIS and ship illustration by Jean Boudriot; p. 12 (inset) © Victoria & Albert
 Museum; p. 16 (gun, cutlass) © National Maritime Museum Picture Library; p. 19 © FPG International; p
  19 (inset) © The Art Archives/Gunshots.

  Weintraub, Aileen, 1973–
    Anne Bonny and Mary Read / Aileen Weintraub. –1st ed.
      p. cm. – (The library of pirates)
  ISBN 0-8239-5795-0 (lib. bdg.)
  1. Bonny, Anne, b. 1700—Juvenile literature. 2. Read, Mary, d. 1720?—Juvenile literature. 3.
  Women Pirates—Caribbean Sea—Biography—Juvenile literature. [1. Bonny, Anne, b. 1700. 2. Read,
  Mary, d. 1720? 3. Pirates. 4. Women—Biography.] I. Title.
    G535 .W42 2002
    917.2904'53—dc21

                                                                    00-012197

 Manufactured in the United States of America

Contents

Famous Female Pirates

Anne Bonny and Mary Read are two of the most **infamous** female pirates of all time. Both women were born in the late seventeenth century. They lived during the Golden Age of Piracy. This was a time during the eighteenth century when European countries still were claiming land in North and South America. The high seas weren't **patrolled** well. This gave pirates plenty of chances to steal and **plunder** trade ships. Anne and Mary sailed the Caribbean Sea as pirates from about 1719 to 1721. However, the world of piracy was usually left to men. It even was considered bad luck to have women on a pirate ship. So how did these women become such fearsome pirates?

◀ *This image shows Anne Bonny and Mary Read in men's clothing. The map at the bottom shows Ireland, where Anne was born, and England, where Mary was born.*

Anne's Childhood

Anne and Mary did not meet until they were adults. As children, though, they both were forced to dress as boys. Anne's father, a lawyer named William Cormac, was married to a rich woman. He left his wife to live with a woman named Mary "Peg" Brennan. Cormac's wife kept giving him money. Soon Cormac and Brennan had Anne. Cormac wanted to keep getting money from his wife, but he knew that she would be mad if she found out about Anne.

Cormac dressed Anne as a boy and told everbody that "he" was a relative who had come to train as a **clerk**. Anne wasn't good at pretending to be a boy. Cormac's wife found out Anne's secret and stopped sending money.

Above Right: This is a picture of a wealthy Frenchman from the late 1700s. ▶

When William Cormac stopped getting money from his wife,
he moved his new family to South Carolina.

Mary dressed as a boy when she worked as a
servant in a French household.

Mary's Childhood

Mary's childhood was very similar to Anne's. Mary's mother married a man and had a baby boy. Soon the man went to sea to earn a living. Mary's mother met another man and soon became pregnant again. She left town to have her baby somewhere else. During this time, her son died. When Mary was born, her mother pretended that the baby was the son who had died. She dressed the baby as a boy and brought the child to her mother-in-law. The mother-in-law supported Mary until she was 13, all the while thinking that Mary was her grandson. At 13, Mary started working as a **footboy** for a French lady.

◀ *Above Left: This picture shows an eighteenth-century woman dressed in French-style clothes.*

Off to Sea

When Anne grew up, she married a sailor named James Bonny. Anne's father did not like her husband and stopped giving her money. Soon Anne's need for adventure got the best of her. She left her husband and went to sea dressed in men's clothing.

About the same time, Mary joined the **military**. She continued to dress like a man. In the service, she fell in love with one of the officers. She told him her secret and they got married. They quit the service and opened a restaurant called The Three Horse Shoes. When her husband suddenly died, Mary started dressing like a man again and boarded a ship headed for the West Indies.

After Mary's husband died, she joined a ship sailing from Europe to the West Indies. This is a map of Europe from 1826, about 100 years after Mary's time. ▶

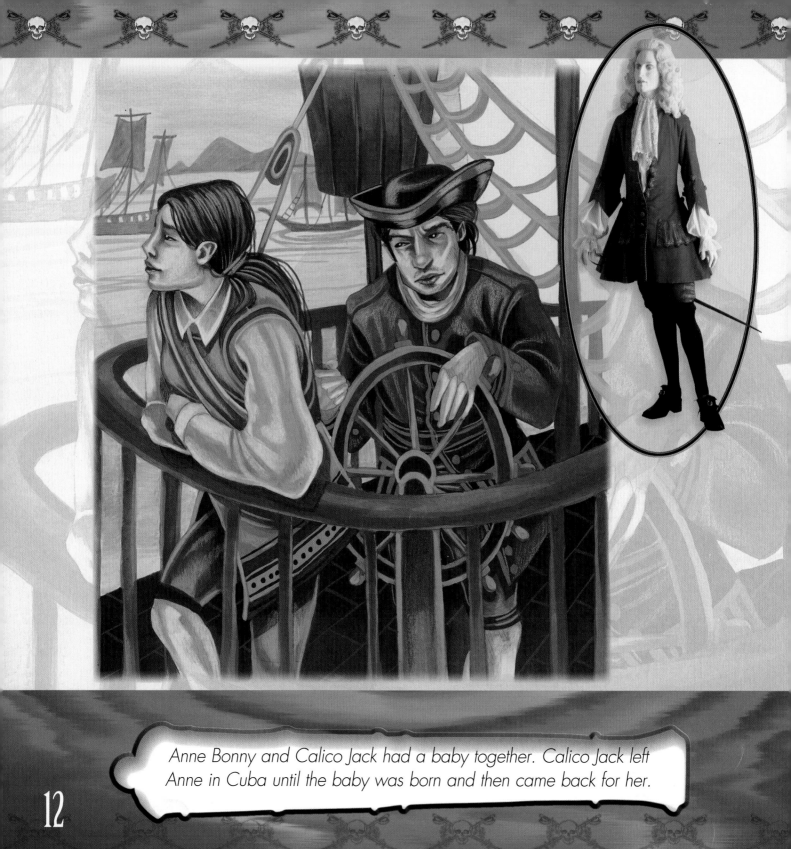

Anne Bonny and Calico Jack had a baby together. Calico Jack left
Anne in Cuba until the baby was born and then came back for her.

Calico Jack

English pirates attacked the ship on which Mary was sailing. The pirates plundered the ship and captured the crew. Thinking she was a man, they told Mary that she would be allowed to live if she signed on as a pirate. Calico Jack was the captain of the ship. His real name was John Rackham. He was called Calico because of the brightly colored clothes he liked to wear. He was known for plundering small ships in and around Jamaica. Even though it was against the rules to have women aboard a pirate ship, Calico Jack decided to let the woman he loved sail with him. She dressed like a man so that others would not know there was a woman aboard. This woman was Anne Bonny.

◀ *The picture on the near left shows what Anne might have worn as a child, when her father dressed her as a boy.*

Anne and Mary Meet

Anne and Mary had to make sure that the other pirates didn't find out they were women. They dressed in **trousers** and men's jackets. They also tied handkerchiefs around their heads. Mary was good at keeping her secret. Anne, on the other hand, didn't try too hard to keep others from finding out the truth. Anne started spending a lot of time with Mary, thinking that Mary was a man. Mary finally told Anne that she was a woman. Anne was happy to have a female friend aboard. Calico Jack became jealous that the two women were spending so much time together. He thought Mary was trying to steal Anne away from him. The women decided to tell Calico Jack the truth.

Anne and Mary had to work hard to keep the crew from finding out they were women because there ▶ was very little privacy on a pirate ship.

Hunting for Pirates

On August 22, 1720, Calico Jack and his crew stole a ship called the *William* from a **harbor** in New Providence. When Captain Roger Woodes, governor of the Bahamas, found out, he sent a ship with 45 men to catch the pirates. Then he sent another ship loaded with weapons and 54 more men to join the hunt. Meanwhile, Calico Jack and his crew continued to attack fishing boats off Harbor Island in the Bahamas. Then they headed to Negril Point in Jamaica. Captain Jonathan Barnet was sailing one of the naval ships. It was nighttime when Barnet finally caught up with Calico's ship. Barnet ordered the pirates to **surrender**.

Pirate ships often were attacked by other pirates or naval ships trying to put an end to piracy. The guns shown here ▶ *have two barrels and are called blunderbusses.*

After being captured, Calico's crew was brought
to Davis Cove in Jamaica.

Not Without a Fight

Calico Jack's crew refused to surrender and began firing their weapons. Barnet fired back and was able to damage Calico Jack's ship. Barnet and his crew boarded the *William*. All but three pirates fled below deck to hide. Two of the pirates that refused to surrender were Anne and Mary. Mary yelled at the pirates to come above deck and fight like men. When they didn't answer, she fired her gun at them, killing one and wounding others. It was no use. Anne and Mary were no match for Barnet's crew. All 18 members of Calico Jack's crew were captured and put on trial.

Death and Disappearance

On November 16, 1720, Calico Jack and most of his male crew were sentenced to death by hanging. The last time Anne saw Calico Jack, she told him that if he had fought like a man, he need not hang like a dog. On November 28, Anne and Mary were tried and sentenced to death. Both Anne and Mary told the court they were pregnant. The decision to kill the two women was put off until they had their babies. Mary died of a fever in prison shortly after being tried. She was buried on April 28, 1721. As for Anne, nobody knows what happened to her. She disappeared from all records. If she survived, she still had her whole life ahead of her. At their trial, both women were no more than twenty-two years old.

Glossary

clerk (KLERK) Someone whose job it is to do general office work.

cutlasses (KUHT-les-es) Short, curved swords.

duel (DOO-el) A fight between two people involving weapons.

footboy (FUT-boy) A serving boy.

harbor (HAR-bor) A protected body of water where ships anchor.

infamous (IN-feh-mes) Having a bad reputation.

military (MIH-lih-ter-ee) Part of a government that protects a country, such as the army or navy.

patrolled (puh-TROHLD) When an area has been guarded to make sure it is safe.

plunder (PLUN-der) To rob by force.

surrender (suh-REN-der) To give up.

trousers (TROW-zers) A type of pants worn by men.

vicious (VIH-shus) Being dangerous and mean.

Index

Web Sites

To learn more about Anne Bonny and Mary Read, check out these Web sites:
http://school.discovery.com/homeworkhelp/worldbook/atozhistory/p/
   432060.html
www.cwrl.utexas.edu/~mchorost/cyberspace/paper3/wiley/bonny.htm
www.powerup.com.au/~glen/anne.htm